Phone Bells Keep Ringing for Me

Choi Seungja

TRANSLATED BY

Won-Chung Kim and Cathy Park Hong

EDITED BY

Joyelle McSweeney

2020 Action Books
Notre Dame, Indiana

Action Books
Joyelle McSweeney and Johannes Göransson, Founding Editors
Katherine Hedeen and Paul Cunningham, Managing Editors
Maxime Berclaz, Sebastian Bostwick, and Natasha Ali, 2018-2020 Editorial Assistants
PJ Lombardo, Jasmine Ortiz, and Valerie Vargas, 2019-2021 Editorial Assistants
Jeffrey Angles, Daniel Borzutzky, Don Mee Choi, Advisory Board
Andrew Shuta, Book Design

Cover photo credit: Kim Sinyong

First Edition

Action Books gratefully acknowledges the support of Daesan Foundation in the translation and publication of this book.

ISBN 978-0-900575-02-0
Library of Congress Control Number: 2019955556

Action Books, 233 Decio Hall, University of Notre Dame, IN, 46556 USA

actionbooks.org

Contents

Three

Four

Five

Phone Bells Keep Ringing for Me

PREFACE

Choi Seungja is one of the most influential feminist poets in South Korea. Born in 1952, Choi emerged as a poet during the 1980s, a turbulent and violent decade which saw nationwide democracy movements against the authoritarian government. During that era, South Korean poets were predominantly populist, writing "people's poetry" that protested authoritarian rule. These poets were also mostly men. But during that time, a new wave of feminist poets emerged, such as Kim Hyesoon, Ko Jung-hee, Kim Seung-hee, and Choi herself. When Choi first started publishing in 1979, her provocative poetry was dismissed by the male literary establishment who expected women to write quiet, domestic poems. As the translator and poet Don Mee Choi writes in the anthology *Anxiety of Words,* Choi's language and content were "attacked for being too rough and vulgar for a female poet."

Born in the small rural town of Yeonki, Choi Seungja attended Korea University, devoting her studies to German Literature, and afterwards made a living as a translator of German- and English-language books. In 1979, she was the first woman poet to publish in the prestigious journal *Literature and Intellect.* Despite her growing success as a poet over the following decades, Choi mostly lived alone in near poverty. In 2001, she experienced a mental illness that kept her in and out of hospitals. A community of poets came to her financial aid to help lift her out of poverty. The poet Kim Hyesoon, for instance, collected money each month to support Choi and the press Munhakdongne gave her a writing space in their office so she had a place to write and translate.

Choi's stripped-down poetry is breathtaking and frightening. Her poems are uncompromising because she will stare into the infinite

1

dark tunnel of her solitude and not break that stare. She writes, with terrifying alacrity, the existential despair of living in a hierarchical society where free will is a joke. While it has been changing, South Korea was a paternalistic and Confucian society, where the individual was subsumed by their family unit, especially for a woman, whose worth was measured by her husband and children. When a woman marries, her name is no longer used. She is called "So-and-so's wife" or "so-and-so's mother." Because Choi was a single woman, she was an aberration. The *I* in her poems is often abjectly alone. The phone in her home is so silent day after day that when it finally rings, she is frightened. Instead of the timeline of a traditional Korean woman who measures her milestones by marriage and children, she only has death to shadow her as she ages. In her poem "Thirty Years Old," Choi writes, "Death's traffic light blinks red / in my two eye sockets / my blood is jelly, my fingernails sawdust, / and my hair wire." In the poem "Already I," Choi contends:

> Already I was nothing:
> mold formed on stale bread,
> trail of piss stains on the wall,
> a maggot-covered corpse
> a thousand years old.
>
> Nobody raised me.
> I was nothing from the beginning,
> sleeping in a rat's hole,
> nibbling on the flea's liver,
> dying absentmindedly. in any old place.
>
> So don't say you know me
> when we cross paths
> like falling stars.
> Idon'tknowyou, Idon'tknowyou,
> You, thou, there, Happiness,
> You, thou, there, Love.

That I am alive
is no more than an endless
rumor.

Metonyms of the body as waste pervade her poetry: the piss, shit,
and vomit that the body rejects and that we recoil from because the
emissions remind us of our own mortality. The barren womb is also a
central motif, evoking the disgrace she feels as a childless woman in a
society where a woman is the sum of her children. It is also a metaphor
of the motherland whose soul has become corrupted by capitalism.
Capitalism has become the only logic that rules her nation, where
all human relationships are mediated by money. The citizen does not
act but is acted upon. In the poem "The Portrait of Mr. Pon Kagya,"
the salaryman Mr. Pon Kagya does not sit on the chair but the chair
sits on him; the pen grips him; the pay envelope thrusts him in his
pocket. Objects have become subjects who have their way with this
salaryman, who is powerless. While Choi's poems may be despairing,
they are simultaneously liberating because she writes in a language
both ruthlessly direct and strangely surreal. She does not obfuscate her
despair with elegant metaphors but confronts it with nightmarishly
strange imagery. In her brutal investigation of her own pain and agony,
she cries out for an alternate way of life.

Choi took a hiatus from poetry in 2001 because of her mental illness,
but her reputation as a formidable poet in South Korea has only grown.
She has published eight books of poetry: *Love in This Age* (1981), *A
Happy Diary* (1984), *The House of Memory* (1989), *My Grave Is Green*
(1993), *Lovers* (1999), *Alone and Away* (2010), *Written on the Water*
(2011), and *Empty Like an Empty Boat* (2016). Choi has also translated
many books into Korean including Friedrich Nietzsche's *Thus Spake
Zarathustra*, Max Picard's *The World of Silence*, Paul Auster's *The Art of
Hunger*, and Erich Fromm's *The Art of Being*. In 1994 she participated
in the International Writing Program at the University of Iowa.

She has received the Daesan Literary Award (2010) and Jirisan Literary Award (2010) and is now regarded as one of the most important poets in Korea.

Cathy Park Hong
New York City
September 2019

One

Already I

Already I was nothing:
mold formed on stale bread,
trail of piss stains on the wall,
a maggot-covered corpse
a thousand years old.

Nobody raised me.
I was nothing from the beginning,
sleeping in a rat's hole,
nibbling on the flea's liver,
dying absentmindedly, in any old place.

So don't say you know me
when we cross paths
like falling stars.
Idon'tknowyou, Idon'tknow you,
You, thou, there, Happiness
You, thou, there, Love.

That I am alive
is no more than an endless
rumor.

Dog Autumn

Dog autumn attacks.
Syphilis autumn.
And death visits
one of twilight's paralyzed legs.

Everything dries out
and all roads' boundaries blur.
The old singer's voice
droops on the recording.

"Hi Jugsun—no? This isn't Jugsun? Jugsun."
In mid-air, the telephone line
loses the receiver, and once-departed lovers
never return, not even in a dream.

In a guest room inside the tavern of time,
where the stagnant waste-water of memory
stinks like horse piss, I ask,
in a voice awakened from disheveled death:
How far have I gone, how far yet to go
before the river becomes the sea?

At Daeheung Temple in Haenam

To Eunji's mom and dad, hoping they read this poem
as a dream of her conception

Deep night, the river flows into the sea,
and our hands search for the hands of our lovers.
The stream sleeping so long in our bodies
suddenly wakes up and flows.

It will rain
across the sea,
soaking your land.

In the valley of the mountain temple
in heaven's empty wine glass
swirls the drunk green wind.
Now, behind a mountain ridge,
the hands of two lovers meet.

Toward You

Like flowing water,
I will come to you.
Like alcohol dissolving in water,
like nicotine congealing in alcohol,
like caffeine coating nicotine,
I will come to you.
Like syphilis germs flowing through veins,
like death gripping life.

Thirty Years Old

When you can't live like this or die like this,
the age of thirty comes.
You wave a white handkerchief painful as a toothache
and beg with the wide-open whites of your eyes.

My dreams are: a cancer cell sprouts in my stomach;
getting married; a poison wide awake
in my liver and intestines.
Death's trafffic light blinks red
in my two eye sockets
my blood is jelly, my fingernails sawdust,
and my hair wire.
A disembodied shade goes forth
through the endless mineral fog,
while birds with no new dreams dream
of flying to memory's Golgotha
to bury their bones.
A white handkerchief drops
and the eyes shutter up their white glare.

Oh, happy happy happy surrender,
shameless-faced, we are happy.

Do You Remember Cheongpa-dong

You were tender during winter.
While the white hand of snow touched our sleep,
we folded up like petals
and wandered the warm earth.

Spring came and you left.
Lilacs bloomed like ghosts
but you didn't smile, even from that far place.
Your glance often made the noise of crumpled cellophane
and your voice stung me like an iron rod.
Yes, for so long, I have been stung in silence.

Even if I have to crawl like a worm with my stung body,
I want to go to you.
I want to steal into your warm light
and be stung for the last time
and die forever.

and now, while I wander the empty field
like worn-out shoes no one claims,
do you remember Cheongpa-dong

and the winter of a few centuries ago
when we folded like petals
and wandered snow-covered dreams?

To Not Be Lonely

To not be lonely,
I eat a lot.
To not be in pain,
I have a little drink.
To not dream,
I swallow sleeping pills.
Finally, I turn off
the switch to my brain.

All night, only the clock's sound
paces the empty room.
Listen carefully:
saddened by indifferent absence,
my shoes collapse and cry.

Love in This Age

In March, no master answers when called to.
At the foot of Dongdaemun Gate, the grass is wet with secrets.

In the unchanging alley,
we slip nimbly into our house
and fall into a sleep that's outside this world.
You call out from the dream's deep mire,
but, my love, the four-thousand-year-old sky's hue is so heavy
we are a cloud whose feet are bound
by "the falling flowers and flowing waters of this country."

We can't decipher
the hot secret codes of these days
through which masked winds call us outside every night,
the terrible love of this age
in which death is followed by another death.

The Hand I Love

Over there, the unknowable rain falls,
miserable rest falls and soaks me.
When I say *I love you* and grab your hand,
the loneliness of existence hangs on my ten fingers.
Over there, the unknowable rain falls,
pitiful peace falls and soaks me.

A Self-Portrait

I'm nobody's disciple,
nobody's friend.
I'm a body seized by premonition,
a daughter of darkness dreaming
in weeds, in a bog.

Mother, I'm darkness.
Since that morning of old
when Adam and Eve rose
from the grassy thicket,
I'm sorrow's long body.

On the shining street,
children sing like birds
and bloom like flowers.
In the sunlight, people of heavenly nature
shine bright,
but I cannot taste their mild wine
with my forked tongue.
I coil myself among the weeds or within a bog,
I wait for sorrow's poison to ferment
throughout my body.

Like a baby inside a womb,
yearning for a mother's love,
I dream the evil dream of the sun
secretly crying out to the sky.

To You

The heart flows more easily than the wind.
Touching the tip of your branch,
I wish I could slip
into your heart
to become the eye
of a never-ending storm.

Anxiety

The hushed sound of poling a boat
washes over the deep night's sky.
Death aims at me
from the invisible sky.
Young dreams hide in the grassy thicket.
Leaves of grass sway all at once
and leak sticky sap.
Stars begin to drip a white, cooled sweat.
Ping! Death fires at me
and fragments of matter flood my ears.
The mouth of darkness flutters for awhile.
Look! The moon, red as crow meat,
shakes the sky.

Women and Men

—for Jeongsuk Kim

Love always comes
like a lightning bolt
and cuts off like a blackout.
Separation comes
as a sudden hunger.

A man's teardrop
is swallowed into the vast sea of his retina.
It's all over, when he turns his back.
Men drift away like a tide,

but women spill out their brain of white loneliness
and turn to the wind
so they can forget.

At twilight, after a long cry
and a few glasses of wine on an empty stomach,
love floats up suddenly and giggles—
the chaos of longing.

Under the drifting stars
on the dirty roofs of this city,
women and men rest their heads
on each other's graves,
vigorously wash and hang up their pasts
that will go soggy again tomorrow.

Two

Phone Bells Keep Ringing for Me

Most people drifted away.
They carried on their backs their desires and sorrows, their desire's dreck.
They flew by my window.
But I didn't drift away.

I didn't drift away.
I mixed desire with despair
and produced one day
and one year,
faithfully paying death's monthly installments.

Yes, phone bells rang endlessly for me,
and I didn't want to avoid the call.
Even if I sank into the pit,
I wanted to touch
my fate.

But I also kept shutting and locking the door,
along with my ears and eyes.
I became a machine of sheer, conditioned reflex.
I called for food in the morning
and pushed sleep into me at night.

Sky's helmsman, you old nihilist
who operates the huge machine of nothingness
in the vacant lot of the sky:
Who will tire first, you or me?
(Of course you know the result,
and even the fact that I created you.)

Phone bells kept ringing for me.
Your mouth was hanging at the end of the phone line,
looking like a cave, a rotten swamp.
From there, death will call for me decisively

and I will answer decisively.
The burning fuse of my fate
will explode in your rotten mouth
completing, in vain, the vanity of all vanities,
useless for thirty years.

Old nihilist, you'll erupt with a bloody, hearty laugh,
and begin to operate, silently, the machine of nothingness
with your old body,
to say that you've completed, in vain,
the vanity of all vanities,
useless for thousands of years.

Sleep Comes Without Its Owner

Sleep comes without its owner
and sleepless night wanders again.
Children, is this poetry or raw rice wine?
The liquor I drank in the winter
gets me drunk in the spring
and I drift away.

Don't hold onto me.
I'm not your mother,
not your child.

Well, I will go all alone
with my old body soaked in poetry and blood.
Clean water laps against every story
of the brightly-lit high-rise buildings.
Saying *not yet, not yet,*
hope crawls until its belly skin
becomes the skin of the earth
and I will arrive at my own grave someday.
Raising merry maggots in the coffin,
I will awake, clean at last,
and start to sing alone.

I Don't Feel Like Eating Dinner Today

Since I don't want to eat my dinner tonight
and be alive the next morning,
I'll collapse where I am and fall asleep.
I'll sleep with nobody knowing.
Though I want to sleep and die,
my spirit, having no place to lie,
frequently slips out of the house and snoops in each alley.
Light pours down bloodily like deboned meat.
Oh, are you still alive today?
Are you alive roaming aimlessly?
From the window of a neon house, where chestnut leaves
tangle like thread snakes and chestnut flowers
burn brightly, I peer out like an orphan:
hearts beating warmly inside a love that can explode
any minute, men and women buzzing around in peace,
resting their heads on their lover's belly
swollen like a cloud.
But what's the point!
On the night street, stars, drunk with smog, shed tears
and the sad night air sings farewell tunes.
Should I wear bright red lipstick in the late fall
and deliver a robust baby next year,
or should I start fasting tomorrow?
When I return and open the door to my room,
death, my pimp, lies down before I do
and stares at me with his two blank eyes
in reply or in revenge.

So On a Certain Day, Love

With a spoonful of steamed rice and a teardrop,
how can I ever fill myself,
eating just this rice mixed with tears?

No matter how much you may love me,
or how much I may love you,
I still have to chew today's chicken
and swallow today's tears.

So let us no longer speak metaphorically.
Everything is concrete as cement
and everything is a cement wall.
What matters are not metaphors but fists,
and fists being smashed.

So don't try to attain what can't be attained
and don't say you've attained the vanity of all vanities.

Go away, love or lover.
To love is not to die for you.
To love is to live
for you
and wait
only to be snapped off
mercilessly.

So, on a certain day, love,
please break my body
snap off my arms and legs

and
arrange
them
in
your
vase.

Spring

Spring comes
even if you don't want it to.
Spring of the lonely, unmarried, thirty-three-year-old woman,
spring of the unemployed,
spring of the taxpayer.

In the spring, plants and grass bloom,
and even garbage grows fresh.
The trash pile grows bigger in my mouth.
I cannot swallow it or vomit it up.
Dump trucks endlessly drive in and out
to unload plastics, scrap iron, dirt, sweat, and shit
into my throat—
already,
unbelievably,
miraculously
elongated like a tunnel.

My Lord, your time has come   .
I can no longer pronounce those words,
and only my hole full of trash
stays afloat in the sky
as if it will be torn
or burst open.

I Have Been to the Sea in Winter

I have been to the sea in winter.
Seagulls honked and freely shat their white droppings,
and a woman's body, drifting along the sea for three days,
was hauled in by the Coast Guard patrol boat.
Her womb was exposed to the sea
(the sea was contaminated).
From her open womb, pale, sick children,
dazed from the trembling sea's sunlight, poured out.
Riding the foaming tide,
children scattered into the five seas and six continents.
Turned into a slippery empty rind,
the dead woman floated like a piece of vinyl.
The children who have scattered into every corner of the world
will build a sturdy cobweb at Pietermaritzburg
or Odendaalsrust in South Africa, lay their eggs
 inside the earth of the Philippine jungles,
and spread syphilis or deliver stillborn babies
under the cover of darkness in Berlin, or on the Rue d'Orchampt
or on Boulevard Haussmann. Now and then,
they might start a revolution in the very long tedious night—
a revolution always destined to misfire.
I have been to the sea in winter.
(The sea was contaminated.)

The Portrait of Mr. Pon Kagya

At nine, the office door cheerfully opens Mr. Pon Kagya.
The chair walks over and sits on Mr. Pon Kagya.
A ballpoint pen rudely grips his finger
and letters stare angrily at him.

At noon, lunch devours him
and urine lazily releases him whenever it wants.
The phone sometimes calls him to kill time.
Hello? Hello! (a hiccup of existence).
Sometimes time passes, other times time does not,
until a pay envelope thrusts him into a pocket.
At six-thirty, the number 54 bus rides him again.
Wonhyo Bridge runs over him again.

The front door opens to push him in.
The warm floor knocks him down.
Sleep begins to gnaw at him.
But at last, in a dream,
the Republic of Korea passionately praises him
and sets up a monument
at the center of Yeouido Square.
A grand chorus rings out—
Worship and praise him!

A Happy Diary

I am happy today. Mother got a clean bill of health. I received the delayed payment for my translation work and this afternoon I was introduced to a modest-looking man at a gathering.

Also, today, balloons sold like hot cakes at Yeouido's riverside; under the night sky of the Gaenari apartments at Dogok-dong, the Moon called out to the Stars to sit and treated them to a cup of beer. Yellow tulips burst out laughing in the retina of Kirin, who is sleeping with a *Bongbong* cracker in his mouth, and the Hundai Pony runs well without gas in Kirin's mother's dream, and wings have secretly grown by one centimeter in the armpits of Kirin's tired father.

Today, I truly want to give thanks to Mr. Star, Soyeong's uncle. Since you've loved our cousins so much, we've dreamt nice dreams and played well under the old, faithful blue sky of Korea.

     Assarabia.
     Doroamitabul.

On Woman

Every woman has a grave inside
where death and birth sweat it out.
All humans struggle to flee
from this eternally blind port.
Women lie down like a rigid dead sea,
like the Altamira Cave or a ruined great shrine.
They provide a home for birds.
Inside the women, where sandwind blows,
broken shells birds have pecked their way out of
and death's debris
are piled high like empty casings.
Everything has to pass through the ruined shrine
and rigid dead sea
in order to be born again
and to die again.

For Y

You have abandoned me.
Saying it's time to break up,
you have abandoned me.
In the mountain and at the seashore,
I have abandoned myself.

When I splayed myself on the table and spread my legs,
I saw the sky through the concrete roof
and the air filling up the lungs of flying birds.

Before I could count to five,
I could no longer see the roof, the sky, and the birds.
While dying, I saw my baby and me
floating endlessly down the city ditch,
down the city ditch and into the womb
of bygone days.

Since then, when I lie down in this world as in a grave
and long for the sky,
my baby flies by,
trailing fins that look like a tadpole's tail.
You bastard, I'll kill you by any means.
I'll give birth to you inside me again.

When my baby, blown by a strong wind,
plunges into the ground,
it lives warm in my grave for a few months
and then departs for the cold sky-sea again,
trailing fins that look like a tadpole's tail.
Oh, son of a bitch,
I'll never forget you!

The Vicious Circle

The world was essentially fear to me.
I was a rat thinking I was a rat in a trap.
a frightened rat baring its teeth
and snapping in advance,
before fear could swallow me,
hoping the world wouldn't swallow me up
just because of my behavior...

Oh, a rat who bites the tail of a rat who bites the tail
of a rat who bites the tail of a rat who bites the tail...

Release

As apples fall in autumn,
the face of someone I know is buried underground.
Battling over whether or not the time goes well or badly,
two pantlegs become threadbare.

Hey, who is that over there,
who waits at my door
throughout my life.

Now that at last I know you aren't my enemy,
come inside me whenever you want.

Three

A Port in the West

The setting sun casts its anchor.

Trailing bones of burning arthritis, I have made it this far—
a port in the West.

Shake me, shake me up!
Neither martyrdom nor apostasy can save me at this age.
When the ships of silence take root in the sea,
please shake up my life,
shake up my whole life!

A Portrait of the Marginal Man

Though he always learns the grammar of this world,
he forgets it all the time.
He cannot judge
if the world is anesthetized
or his own brain is anesthetized.
He knows too well, but sometimes doesn't know at all,
how material travels through a passage into spirituality
or spirit into materiality.

By habit, the marginal man waits anxiously
for the hour the newspaper is delivered
and the TV begins broadcasting.
He sometimes dials 116 to check
if the only clock in his home is correct
and listens to the robot voice read its sentence
to the end.

He usually travels
by subway or intercity bus.
Sometimes he risks his life
and takes a bullet taxi.
Jealous of those happy men
who believe in the ideology of happiness,
missing the bouncy surface tension of Seoul,
endlessly craving and hating being immersed in it,
wandering aimlessly from surface to surface,
outskirt to outskirt,
edge to edge,
he makes a mess of the map with his randomness
and rolls around, endlessly mixing up times.

Come Back, Now

Birds always sink lower and lower,
and disheveled longing calls me from outside,
always from outside.

Between the restless ripples, I have danced
for too long.

Now, I think I have to leave you.

Ohwa, ohwa! Our sorrow
has rowed this far.

Abandoning you in the vast water,
I have to leave you now.

The star that sank deep into my eyes long ago
rises again. Blood circulates again
in the land of my long longing.
I come back and mend the fence.

How shabby it is!
Weeds have already grown
taller than me.

The House of Destruction

Wind from all directions, the sound of wind.
The house besieged by waves of wind.
The age of 37 has nowhere to rest.

Absent dreaming and present reality,
between them, the wind—
the sound of wind shakes me.

The room in the air, the hollow house
forever rootless.

Vain and futile,
I destroy this house.
Do not restore it,
and never build a memorial over it.
In name and in reality, this is the house of destruction.

Dance of Agony

The world monopolized by wind—
a fleet of strong wind,
a school of blue-backed, man-eating sharks.

My kidney swells by instinct.
I have a hunch
that tonight's fight will be a close one.

So now the dazzling dance
of agony begins.
Sorrow, watch
how I dance
to your rhythm,
look at my supple arms and legs.
For all my life,
how well my body
has grown used to your rhythm.

Poetry, or Charting a Way

Well, courageously I arrive at a thought
that may be abandoned again.
Even so, poetry is a way.
But the way is not opened yet
and I have to chart it out by myself.
Yes, poetry is charting a way.
I have to chart a way
so I might cross ways with others.

Charting a way
and leaving a trace of the way,
I wish that this way will meet other ways,
and not go too far alone.
I wish someone would follow
close enough that I don't feel lonely.

Having No Way

Having no other way,
I laugh just like a gourd flower.

I am not waiting for an answer,
I am only gazing at myself
who gazes at the white snow
that falls and covers the never-arriving answer.

All things are endurable.
My cells seem to be getting old.
Though I am poor,
this room is cozy.
This running waterway is friendly,
the funeral of water is streaming away.

Please forget me,
since the easiest me to dream of
is me in the grave.

Already, the World

Already, the world
was a gathering of my failings
and a waste heap of my scars.
And so now my blood is all the rainwater flowing
down to some unknown place.

Anyone, call out for me!
From one end of the sea,
madly call out for me!

Then I will scatter cry upon cry
on you like foam.

My poems, short as a shriek,
will spread
over the white horizon.

Lonely Women

Lonely women
wait for the phones to ring— which never ring.
Lonelier women are petrified
when their phones— that have never rung— suddenly ring.
Much lonelier women are afraid
that their phones— that have never rung— may suddenly ring,
and their hearts may stop at that moment.
Still, much lonelier women pretend to be asleep
or actually are asleep when all the world's lovers
call them at once.

At the Winter Field

Love is most beautiful when it surrenders—
whether to the strongest strength
or to the weakest weakness.
Love is most beautiful
when it surrenders.

Sorrow! I sink into it lower and lower
into these fields and woods,
these low mountains and streams.

Please, take
this forehead, feverish for life.

Please, close
these wicked eyes which have seen all
the things they shouldn't have seen.

(Now again, someone starts to cross the field
where no one has passed for a long time.
You should hang this life's wet shadow up to dry,
while there's still enough sun.)

Do You Remember?

Do you remember
the day we first met
when so much water fell for so long,
like joy and like sorrow?

Since you didn't call me,
I couldn't fall asleep.
Since you didn't call me ever again,
I tossed and turned all my life.

It Turns Cloudy

It turns cloudy and, soon after, rain falls.
A few rolling stones stop
and in the small room of worms,
the worms' cry
rings more lonely.

When it rains, do I cry?
The age for lyric is over,
and only the age for
practicing lyrics
remains.

Four

Not Forgetting or Memorandum 1

Nobody will know
how those times passed.
Nobody will tell you
the inside facts of those times.

The years threw heaps of shit at me,
lump after lump,
asking me to live
on shit.

For no reason, the years threw shit
ruthlessly in front of me and behind me,
into my mind and my body, too.
Those unchanging years
which couldn't even flow away
fed me shit
and left me mercilessly
alive.

Not Forgetting or Memorandum 2

I keep my five organs always shut tight
in order not to eat,
not to throw up.
But the waste of my Pavlovian,
auto-repetitive life
is always choked down
and thrown up.

From the beginning,
my life has been a waste.

Not Forgetting or Memorandum 3

At the tip of a shameful branch of life,
the bird of death cries.
At the tip of a futile branch of death,
the bird of life cries.

No one will question
where the bird has gone.
The sky will always be this blue
keeping its secrets
about the ways of leaping and falling.

Feeling a premonition of eventual falling,
rather than landing at last,
the bird soars and flies—
the little bird's bruised feathers
dance between ripples.

Not Forgetting or Memorandum 4

The street brims with presences,
but it also floods with so many absent existences.
As the absences of all those absences,
I have bloomed
like a dark poisonous mushroom.

Because I didn't like to run, my life was late.
Because I didn't like to walk, my life was absent.

Oh all those splendid—
I was absent from,
Oh all those splendid—
places from which
I was absent!
Now I'd like to stretch and lie down on the world,
the shadow of my own absence.

Not Forgetting or Memorandum 6

A mammal always wants to cling,
either with words or flesh.
The sound of footsteps always echoes
in the long corridor of the brain's cinerea—
sound that will never disappear.

Yes, even at this moment, memories,
memories and corpses with tightly shut eyes
drift in rows
down the cold ditch water.
Freighted with memory,
the night boat will sail
wearily again up the River Jordan.

Not Forgetting or Memorandum 8

When my grave
goes greener and greener
until, swallowed in greenness,
its trace is finally gone,
then, at last,
streams will brim with a lovely watery sound
and roads will be full of meditation's silence.
Then, finally, won't a road of death-in-life or life-in-death
open anew?

Not Forgetting or Memorandum 10

Sorrow, I'd like to see your face
and your features.

(I wonder what the face of sorrow in this age is made of.
I don't know why stones of sorrow crunch so much
on the road one person or one age walks.)

Sorrow, I'd like to see your true features tonight,
even once, even in a dream.

And I want to make a final decision
whether I will kiss your face
or
smear shit on your face.

Not Forgetting or Memorandum 13

When loneliness comes to pierce me like a spear,
what shield should I hold?
Oh, where can I find my shield,
when my whole body and soul are a shield?

It is a shield of immortality,
resurrection, a new life,
until the day death's companion, loneliness,
comes to visit me.

Therefore, let's prepare enough blood today
to pour out before the spear of loneliness,
for my blood will always suffice for as long as I live.

The Tribe of Capital

In this age, in which a poem a few lines long
can flutter suddenly like a handful of 10,000 won bills,
an age in which dung can be an art, and a commodity,
let's write that stuff,
tha-a-a-a-a-a-a-a-a-a-t stuff.
The Spirit is an angel you can find in a children's book.

In this world (covered by the tribe of capital),
where money mothers give birth to money babies
and capital mothers, capital babies,
I will raise capital kids into mothers,
if the baby of the baby of the baby of capital can be a poem
(all poets, lie prostrate).
I will make them higher-order capital animals
(like the Aryan tribe), surpassing even that higher-order mammal
called the human.

The capital animal floods everywhere
and humans whom we know all too well
are changing into the class Reptilia in the tribe of capital.
It is sad to see the snakeskin pattern imprinted on my arm.
The day will come when even birds cry *capital, capital*.

(Teach me a postmodern way;
I don't know why I can only talk in this traditional way.)

The Age of 40

Turning 30 was like standing at the edge of a high cliff.
After that, I thought, my steps would be like one long descent,
like falling endlessly down a deep hill.
But my 40s form a vast plane like a huge vault,
so wide I can't see its walls
or downward slopes, no matter how far I walk.
Yet sheer glass walls stand here and there at random
and I'll knock my head against them, if I'm unlucky.

But I have one thing I believe firmly
and live by, every day of my 40s:
In trust is treason.

The End of a Century

The 1970s were a horror
and the 1980s a humiliation.
Now, what stigma will the end of this century stick to me?

Limitation leads to a cliff.
The cliff grips the sea.

I wish I had a friend
to beat me like a dog
when I get upset.
Oh, I wish I'd become a dog, beaten to death.
I'd like to become a carpet made of the skin of a dog
beaten to death. In the twenty-first century,
I'd like to be a rag, trodden by your feet.
(Please trod on me softly).

To You

I wish you'd come to me.
I'm fatal.
I don't have anything to sell
except my own life.

This world in which I have nothing to sell except my life:
rain comes, wind blows, and snow falls over my window,
looking like a desolate shop window.
I'm fatal.

I have nothing more to sell you,
and to the world either.
The shop window of my soul is completely empty.
Only my neck, completely drained and stuffed,
hangs like a portrait of a dead king.

I wish you'd come to me.
They say I'm fatal.

Five

A White Day Moon

A white day moon,
a blue roc.
The sky tires,
travelling a long and distant road.

Setting a few specks of blue roc afloat,
the sky limps on.

Between Lao-tzu and Chang-tzu

How can I dance this dance
between Lao-tzu and Chang-tzu?
One is too taciturn
and the other too chatty,
yet, as if by agreement,
they don't say a thing
about the essence of mysticism.
Lao-tzu's dance is a monk's dance
while Chang-tzu's is a mask dance,
and I don't know which dance to dance.
I have not even touched one
and barely grazed the other
for an instant as brief as my little finger.
Between the sea of Lao-tzu and Mount Tai of Chang-tzu,
what dance will I dance?

(I hear two rabbis
pass close and greet each other
in heaven.)

Travel Light

You change easily, like the wind.
Now a flower, now a rock,
now a poem, and now a novel.
Without a backpack, you travel light.
You don't even wear briefs, or trousers, or shoes.

Even when I cry in the dream in which I am absent,
your motto, *travel light,*
carries straight on:
Now a rock, now a flower,
now a novel, and now a poem

without telephone numbers or an address book
(even without consciousness
or unconsciousness).

Alone and Away

This world is a faraway world
where Dongbang Sak lived
for three thousand six-hundred-year cycles.
It is a world where people go away and come back
and go again if they have free time.
This world is a faraway world where Dongbang Sak lived
for three thousand six-hundred-year cycles.
Lao-tzu lived in this world,
Chang-tzu and Jesus, too.
This world is a faraway world
where rain and snow fall today.

(There goes Christianity,
Buddhism,
and Taoism.)

This is a tale— alone and away.

I'll Go, Writing a Piece of Cloud

I'll go, writing a piece of cloud,
the breakfast table, the nothingness in a spoonful of coffee,
the infinity of water in the coffee mug.

(A child is eating
an apple outside the window.
I watch her
savoring
a world.)

Somewhere, birds cry
and the moon sinks.

I'll go, writing a piece of cloud.

Why the World?

What will rot away in the world?

Why does the world
become a world
only once it thoroughly rots?

The big secret
is capital.

Is the world prosperous?
Is it plentiful?

This limber wheel
spins and runs idly.

With nothing else to do,
I stare at the world
that somebody's stared at time and time again.

(Do they say *Kaku Karak* for *Coca-cola*?)

A Buddhist Monk

Waking from a hundred-year sleep,
a monk says
Mind is mind, matter is matter.

For better or worse, when you mix them up,
they become matter-mind
and mind-matter.

When you climb to the top rung of the ladder,
you'll see the calabashes swing brightly.
Mind-matter becomes matter-mind
and vice versa.
(In fact, mind becomes matter
and matter becomes mind.)

If you decide to go on,
they'll stay separate forever.
But if you refuse to continue,
they'll collapse into one.

(On a very melancholy day,
drink a couple cups of milky magkeolli.)

The Gray Shadow of Time

Time is always standing still.

A flower sways
on the other side of centuries.

A *Dasein* — a Heideggerian window— also sways.

Why does the time always stand still
in this ever-swaying world?

In this world, swaying as eternity does,

the gray shadow of time
stands still and leaves no trace.

Another World

We were of one mind, one body.

Peacefully,
cranes fly and bluebirds fall,
between the endless sea and the sea
(Oh, did I sleep too long?)
cranes fly and bluebirds fall.
What has happened?

From where do the others come?
The world made up of other things—
this world existed once, then ended, and now exists again.
I have touched it again and again.
The world exists again, will exist for a billion years,
this world made up of so many other things
as blue as the sea and sky.

My Poetry Is Moving Now

My poetry is moving now.
For too long, the field of my poetry has lain fallow:
too deep a darkness, too solidified a darkness.
Now, I want to move
into a slower house of fluttering green.
But I don't know yet
what kind of house I'll move to.
I hope it's neither on a market street
nor a mountain slope.

I don't want to move
to a-n-o-t-h-e-r field of flowers
but to a field of grass.

It's Time

Some people relive the past as the present.
Since they have no spirit they can dig out and eat,
they mix and eat the past for today's buffet.
When will the day come
when even the spirit runs out?
Some people insist that we have to eat
that spirit buffet together—otherwise, we're not human.
Can we just skip it,
just daydream?
Some people say we even have to boil and eat the stone of the past,
because our spirits are hungry ghosts,
even when the sun sets and moon rises.
For the sake of the past, some people would like to skip
the present as well as the future.
Time passes quickly, tick, tick.

As Eliot says, *It's time, It's time.*

A Cloudy Day

My time, which couldn't be converted to salary or capital,
went off somewhere
and somebody shakes the me who isn't me.
I am not me, but somebody shakes me.
I sway calmly, asking *who am I?*

Does the full moon give birth to the crescent moon
or the crescent moon to the full moon?

To wax and wane is different
from waning while waxing.

Does the full moon give birth to the crescent moon
or the crescent moon to the full moon?

On a day as cloudy as rainwater leaking from the ceiling,
the invisible crescent moon may give birth
to an invisible full moon again.

A Camel Going Alone

Everyone sleeps under the stars.
Exhausted from asking for directions,
he falls asleep on the road.

Everyone sleeps under the stars,
waking death by death.

Therefore, under the starlight,
a camel goes alone.

Under the stars,
it goes without sleep, alone.

In the School of Time

As spacetime expands, the sea expands.
Though the ferry comes and goes,
the sea is still the sea
and the island still the island.

I live on that island,
looking at the sky now and then.

I live in the school of time,
angling for time.

That the sea I have to cross is getting bigger
worries me.

Notes on the Translations

"Love in this Age": "falling flowers and flowing waters" is a phrase traditionally used to denote the passing of Spring.

"So On a Certain Day, Love": Eating steamed rice mixed with water, having no side dishes, indicates a miserable life in Korea.

"A Happy Diary": "Pony" is the first car manufactured in Korea. "Kirin" is the name of a baby. "Assarabia" conveys "yay" or "hooray" while "doroamitabul" conveys an exercise in futility.

"The End of a Century": "Please tread on me softly" : A line in Kim Sowol's "Azalea," one of the most popular Korean poems.

"Alone and Away": Dongbang Sak (Dongbang Shao) was a Han Dynasty scholar-official and court jester to Emperor Wu. According to legend, he lived three thousand sexagenary, because he ate "the peaches of immortality."

"Why the World": *Kaku Karak*: Korean pronunciation of Chinese characters 可口可樂 (Chinese transliteration of *Coca-Cola*).

"A Buddhist Monk" : "magkeolli": Korean raw rice wine.

Acknowledgments

This volume has been compiled from the following titles by Choi Seungja:

Love in This Age (1981)
A Happy Diary (1984)
The House of Memory (1989)
My Grave Is Green (1993)
Alone and Away (2010)

The translation of this project was supported by a generous grant from the Daesan Foundation.

Much gratitude to PEN America, Typo Mag, and Poem-A-Day from the Academy of American Poets for publishing a few of these translations.

We wish to thank Choi Seungja for granting us the rights to translate her extraordinary poems. We also thank Joyelle McSweeney, Johannes Görannson and Don Mee Choi for their edits and generous support.

Choi Seungja is one of the most influential feminist writers in South Korea. Born in 1952, Choi emerged as a poet during the 80s, a turbulent and violent decade which saw nationwide democracy movements against the authoritarian government. She made her literary debut in 1979 and shortly after became an icon of youth and freedom in Korean literature, being dubbed "the common pronoun of the 80s poets." She published *Love in This Age* (1981), *A Happy Diary* (1984), *The House of Memory* (1989), *My Grave Is Green* (1993), and *Lovers* (1999). 2001 saw the inception of a mental illness that has kept her in and out of hospitals ever since. A community of poets and presses, led by the renown poet Kim Hyesoon, came to Choi's aid to help lift her out of poverty and enable her to continue to write. Choi returned to publishing with the volume *Alone and Away* (2010), for which she received the Daesan Literary Award (2010) and Jirisan Literary Award (2010). Her subsequent publications include *Written on the Water* (2011) and *Empty Like an Empty Boat* (2016).

Won-Chung Kim is a professor of English Literature at Sungkyunkwan University in Seoul, South Korea. He received his Ph.D. from the University of Iowa, and has published articles on American ecopoets including Gary Snyder, Wendell Berry, Robinson Jeffers, A.R. Ammons, and W.S. Merwin, in journals such as *ISLE* (*Interdisciplinary Studies of Literature and Environment*), *CLCWeb*, and *Comparative American Studies*. Kim has also translated twelve books of Korean poetry into English, including *Cracking the Shell: Three Korean Ecopoets* and *Heart's Agony: Selected Poems of Chiha Kim*. Kim has co-edited with Simon Estok *East Asian Ecocriticisms: A Critical Reader* (Palgrave Macmillan, 2013). He has also translated John Muir's *My First Summer in the Sierra* and Thoreau's *Natural History Essays* into Korean. His first book of poetry, *I Thought It Was a Door*, was published in 2014.

Cathy Park Hong's latest poetry collection, *Engine Empire*, was published in 2012 by W.W. Norton. Her other collections include *Dance Dance Revolution*, chosen by Adrienne Rich for the Barnard Women Poets Prize,and *Translating Mo'um*. Hong is the recipient of the Windham-Campbell Prize, the Guggenheim Fellowship, and a National Endowment for the Arts Fellowship. Her poems have been published in *Poetry*, *A Public Space, Paris Review*, *McSweeney's*, *Baffler, Boston Review*, *The Nation*, and other journals. She is the poetry editor of the *New Republic* and is a professor at Rutgers-Newark University. Her book of creative nonfiction, *Minor Feelings*, was published by One World/Random House in Spring 2020.